Together Met Together Bound

HYMN SETTINGS

by

William Rowan

Selah Publishing Co.

DEDICATION

To my
FRIEND
Marianne Ploger Hill
whose
TEACHING
glorifies the
MAKER'S
Name

William Rowan
16 May
AD 1993

Copyright © 1993, Selah Publishing Co., Inc. All rights reserved.
ISBN 0-9622553-5-1

Typeset and printed in the United States of America. Calligraphy by William P. Rowan.

 Printed on recycled and acid-free paper

First edition
2 3 4 5 6 7 8 9 10 98 97 96 95 94 93

Foreword

In the hot summer of 1983, during my first visit to the United States, a young musician approached me after a workshop on God-language with an uproarious remake of "All glory, laud, and honor," which delighted the audience and helped educate this particular Englishman in the nuances of American government.

Thus, I met Bill Rowan. It soon became clear that his gentle humor is matched by fine music. His settings of my hymn texts enrich and move me. Later, I came to know him as an excellent teacher, able to share his composition-process with professional colleagues and semi-musicians like myself, in a manner exciting and enlightening. I recommend him highly as clinician and composer, and am honored to be invited to write this brief word.

Brian Wren
May 1993

P.S. In case you're wondering, what Rowan the Bard wrote was:

All honor, praise, and glory,
to you, great President.
Your Word cannot be vetoed
'cos it's divinely sent.

And when your term is over
(this *is* Democracy)
you'll need a good replacement.
Perhaps you'd call on me?
     All honor, praise, and glory....

I'd serve with pomp and splendor;
my praises all would sing.
In fact, I'd tell the Congress,
"You'd better call me King.'"
     All honor, praise, and glory....

Introduction

William P. Rowan is already known to many as a fine contemporary composer of hymn tunes. We are pleased to publish this complete collection of his tunes (though we do expect many more wonderful tunes out of this composer) that have appeared in hymnals, supplements, and other collections, along with many which are published here for the first time.

This collection is arbitrarily organized alphabetically by first line. The complete indexes in the back of the book should allow the user to find hymns for many different topics or scripture passages. It begins with a setting of Fred Pratt Green's "When in Our Music, God Is Glorified," the premise of all of Rowan's work: to glorify God.

You will find here hymns for a great variety of uses in worship, and you will quickly sense Rowan's sensitivity to the texts. His style is as varied as the texts he sets to music, yet all of his hymns are eminently suited for congregational singing. Through these hymns you will be able to sing a new song unto the Lord.

When in Our Music, God Is Glorified

YOGANANDA

10 10 10 with alleluias

1 When, in our mu-sic, God is glo-ri-fied, and a-dor-
2 How of-ten, mak-ing mu-sic, we have found a new di-
3 So has the church, in lit-ur-gy and song, in faith and
4 And did not Je-sus sing a Psalm that night when ut-most
5 Let ev-ery in-stru-ment be tuned for praise. Let all re-

a-tion leaves no room for pride, it is as though the
men-sion in the world of sound, as wor-ship moved us
love, through cen-tu-ries of wrong, borne wit-ness to the
e-vil strove a-gainst the Light? Then let us sing, for
joice who have a voice to raise! And may God give us

whole cre-a-tion cried "Al-le-lu-ia! Al-le-lu-ia!"
to a more pro-found Al-le-lu-ia! Al-le-lu-ia!
truth in ev-ery tongue, Al-le-lu-ia! Al-le-lu-ia!
whom he won the fight: Al-le-lu-ia! Al-le-lu-ia!
faith to sing al-ways Al-le-lu-ia! Al-le-lu-ia!

Text: Fred Pratt Green, 1972. © 1972, Hope Publishing Co. Carol Stream, IL 60188. All rights reserved. Used by permission
Music: William P. Rowan, 1985. © 1991, Selah Publishing Co., Inc. All rights reserved.
Anthem/concertato setting of this hymn: Selah Publishing Co., Inc. (catalog no. 42

A Child, a Woman, and a Man

DURNBAUGH

88 88 888

1 A child, a wo-man, and a man are peo-ple dear and
2 A child, a wo-man, and a man are peo-ple in a
3 For, if I some-how shift the blame for all my pride and
4 Yet Je-sus al-so was re-viled and brand-ed as the
5 Then love us, Je-sus, as you can, un-til we see, con-

close to me; a name, a smile, a voice I
for-eign land, whose word I doubt, whose hopes I
guilt with-in, the for-eign peo-ple Je-sus
en-e-my, the scape-goat who em-braced the
fess, con-demn, more than the e-vil oth-ers

know, a hand I touch, a face I see; and,
fear, whose ways I can-not un-der-stand; and
loves will be the scape-goats for my sin, as
cross in love for all and love for me; and
do, the e-vils we might do to them. Come,

more than I can see or know, I know that Je - sus
yet I need to feel and know how deep - ly Je - sus
they look e - vil, I feel good, and I can right - eous -
when I meet the Lamb of God, I find my - self con -
hu - man - ize our speech and thought till we are look - ing

knows and loves that ve - ry wo - man, child, and man.
knows and loves that ve - ry wo - man, child, and man.
ly de - stroy what Je - sus loves, in Je - sus' name.
vict - ed, loved, for - giv - en, healed, and re - con - ciled.
through your eyes at ev - ery wo - man, child, and man.

Arise, Shine Out, Your Light Has Come

3

BATCHELOR
LM (88 88)

1 A - rise, shine out, your light has come, un - fold - ing Ci - ty
2 A - bove earth's val - leys, thick with night, high on your walls the
3 From walls sur - pas - sing time and space, un - num - bered gates, like
4 The sounds of vi - o - lence shall cease as dwel - lings of sal -
5 The dan - cing air shall glow with light and sun and moon give

of our dreams. On dis - tant hills a glo - ry gleams:
dawn ap - pears, and his - to - ry shall dry its tears,
o - pen hands, shall gath - er gifts from all the lands,
va - tion rise to spar - kle in e - ter - nal skies
up their place when Love shines out of ev - ery face:

Optional Amen after st. 5

the new cre - a - tion has be - gun.
as na - tions stream to - wards your light.
and wel - come all the hu - man race.
from av - e - nues of praise and peace.
our Good, our Glo - ry, our De - light. A - men.

Text: Isaiah 60:1-19, para. by Brian Wren, 1987. © 1989, Hope Publishing Co., Carol Stream, IL 60188.
    All rights reserved. Used by permission.
Music: William P. Rowan, 1993. © 1993, Selah Publishing Co., Inc. All rights reserved.

As We Gather at Your Table

TRUESDELL
87 87 D

4

1 As we gath - er at your Ta - ble, as we lis - ten to your
2 Turn our wor - ship in - to wit - ness in the sac - ra - ment of
3 Gra - cious Spir - it, help us sum - mon oth - er guests to share that

Word, help us know, O God, your pre - sence: let our hearts and minds be
life; send us forth to love and serve you, bring - ing peace where there is
feast where tri - umph - ant Love will wel - come those who had been last and

stirred. Nour - ish us with sac - red sto - ry till we claim it as our
strife. Give us, Christ, your great com - pas - sion to for - give as you for -
least. There no more will en - vy blind us nor will pride our peace des -

own; teach us through this ho - ly ban - quet how to make Love's vic - tory known.
gave; may we still be - hold your im - age in the world you died to save.
troy, as we join with saints and an - gels to re - peat the sound - ing joy.

Text: Carl P. Daw, Jr., 1989. © 1989, Hope Publishing Co., Carol Stream, IL 60188. All rights reserved. Used by permission.
Music: William P. Rowan, 1987. © 1993, Selah Publishing Co., Inc. All rights reserved.

Before the World Had Yet Begun

SEED OF LIFE

LM

1 Be - fore the world had yet be - gun her
2 In that bright dawn - ing of the world, be -
3 Thus, when cre - a - tion's Lord did take the
4 For us, who would this God at - tend, no

jour - ney round the burn - ing sun, be - fore a seed of
fore sea surged or wind un - furled, the vaults of heaven with
clay of earth our form to make, God willed that to our
earth - ly mind can com - pre - hend e - ter - nal glo - ry;

life had stirred, there sound - ed God's cre - a - ting Word.
prais - es rang, the morn - ing stars to - geth - er sang.
race be - long the gifts of mu - sic, word, and song.
praise a - lone is our com - pan - ion on that throne.

Christ Is Risen! Shout Hosanna

JACKSON NEW
87 87 D

1 Christ is ris-en! Shout Ho-san - na! Cel - e - brate this day of days!
2 Christ is ris-en! Raise your spir - its from the cav - erns of de - spair.
3 Christ is ris-en! Earth and heav - en nev - er - more shall be the same.

Christ is ris-en! Hush in won-der: all cre - a - tion is a-mazed.
Walk with glad-ness in the morn-ing. See what love can do and dare.
Break the bread of new cre - a - tion where the world is still in pain.

In the des - ert all-sur-round-ing, see a spread-ing tree has grown.
Drink the wine of res-ur-rec-tion. Not a ser - vant, but a friend,
Tell its grim, de-mon-ic chor-us: "Christ is ris - en! Get you gone!"

Heal - ing leaves of grace a-bound-ing bring a taste of love un-known.
Je - sus is our strong com-pan - ion. Joy and peace shall nev - er end.
God the First and Last is with us. Sing Ho-san - na, ev - ery-one!

Text: Brian Wren, 1984.
Music: William P. Rowan, 1984.

Christ upon the Mountain Peak

FLYNN

78 78 with alleluia

1 Christ up-on the moun-tain peak stands a-lone in glo-ry blaz-ing. Let us, if we dare to speak, with the saints and an-gels praise him— *Al - le - lu - ia!

2 Trem-bling at his feet we saw Mo-ses and E-li-jah speak-ing. All the Proph-ets and the Law shout through them their joy-ful greet-ing— Al - le - lu - ia!

3 Swift the cloud of glo-ry came, God, pro-claim-ing in its thun-der Je-sus as his Son by name! Na-tions, cry a-loud in won-der!— Al - le - lu - ia!

4 This is God's be-lov-ed Son. Law and Pro-phets fade be-fore him, first and last and on-ly One. Let cre-a-tion now a-dore him— Al - le - lu - ia!

* "Let us praise him" may be
substituted for "Alleluia."

Come to Me, O Weary Traveler

AUSTIN
87 87

1 Come to me, O weary traveler; come to me with your distress; come to Me, you heavy bur - dened; come to me and find your rest.

2 Do not fear, my yoke is ea - sy; do not fear, my bur - den's light; do not fear the path be - fore you; do not run from me in fright.

3 Take my yoke and leave your trou - bles; take my yoke and come with me. Take my yoke, I am be - side you; take and learn hu - mil - i - ty.

4 Rest in me, O weary traveler; rest in me and do not fear. Rest in me, my heart is gen - tle; rest and cast a - way your care.

9

For the Fruit of All Creation

RAICA
84 84 88 84

God's Paschal Lamb Is Sacrificed for Us

YOGANANDA

10 10 10 with alleluias

1 God's Pas-chal Lamb is   sac - ri - ficed for us;   there- fore with
2 Now is Christ raised and   will not die a - gain;   death has no
3 In   Christ we   see   the   first fruits of the dead: though A - dam's

joy we keep the   Eas - ter   feast;   for - sak - ing sin,   we
more do - min - ion   o - ver   him.   Through him we   die   to
sin has doomed all flesh to   die,   in Christ's new life   shall

share the bread of   truth. Al - le - lu - ia, al - le - lu - ia!
sin   and live to   God.   Al - le - lu - ia, al - le - lu - ia!
all   be made a -   live.   Al - le - lu - ia, al - le - lu - ia!

10

Glorious the Day

PLOGER

LM with alleluias

1 Glo - rious the day when Christ was born to wear the crown that
2 Glo - rious the day when Christ a - rose, the sur - est friend of
3 Glo - rious the day of Gos - pel grace when Christ re - stores the
4 Glo - rious the day when Christ ful - fills what self re - jects yet

Cae - sars scorn, Al - le - lu - ia! Al - le - lu - ia! Al - le -
all his foes; Al - le - lu - ia! Al - le - lu - ia! Al - le -
fall - en race, Al - le - lu - ia! Al - le - lu - ia! Al - le -
feeb - ly wills; Al - le - lu - ia! Al - le - lu - ia! Al - le -

lu - ia! Al - le - lu - ia! Whose life and death that
lu - ia! Al - le - lu - ia! Who for the sake of
lu - ia! Al - le - lu - ia! When doubt - ers kneel and
lu - ia! Al - le - lu - ia! When that strong light puts

Text: Fred Pratt Green, 1967. © 1969, Hope Publishing Co., Carol Stream, IL 60188.
Music: William P. Rowan, © 1987, Hope Publishing Co., Carol Stream, IL 60188. All rights reserved. Used by permission.

love re - veal which we all need and need to feel: Al - le -
those he grieves tran - scends the world he nev - er leaves; Al - le -
wa - verers stand, and faith a - chieves what rea - son planned; Al - le -
out the sun and all is end - ed, all be - gun; Al - le -

lu - ia! Al - le - lu - ia! Al - le - lu - ia! Al - le - lu - ia!
lu - ia! Al - le - lu - ia! Al - le - lu - ia! Al - le - lu - ia!
lu - ia! Al - le - lu - ia! Al - le - lu - ia! Al - le - lu - ia!
lu - ia! Al - le - lu - ia! Al - le - lu - ia! Al - le - lu - ia!

God of Many Names

MANY NAMES

55 88 D with refrain

Unison

1 God of man - y Names, gath - ered in - to One, in your glo - ry
God of Hov - ering Wings, Womb and Birth of time, joy - ful - ly we
2 God of Jew - ish faith, Ex - o - dus and Law, in your glo - ry
God of Je - sus Christ, Rab - bi of the poor, joy - ful - ly we

come and meet us, Mov - ing, end - less - ly Be - com - ing;
sing your prais - es, Breath of life in ev - ery peo - ple—
come and meet us, joy of Mir - i - am and Mo - ses;
sing your prais - es, cru - ci - fied, a - live for ev - er—

Harmony

Hush, hush, hal - le - lu - jah, hal - le - lu - jah! Shout,

shout, hal - le - lu - jah, hal - le - lu - jah! Sing, sing hal - le -

Text: Brian Wren, 1985.
Music: William P. Rowan, 1986.

lu - jah, hal - le - lu - jah! Sing, God is love, God is love! love!

3 God of Wounded Hands,
    Web and Loom of love,
    in your glory come and meet us,
    Carpenter of new creation;
  God of many Names,
  gathered into One,
  joyfully we sing your praises,
  Moving, endlessly Becoming—
    Hush, hush, hallelujah, hallelujah!...

Go Forth in Faith

LARGENT
11 10 11 10

1 "Go forth in faith, from kin-dred, home, and cus-tom.
2 How hard to trek from ease in Phar-aoh's pal-ace,
3 Yet when we laugh at hope, like Sar-ah, griev-ing
4 With-in the womb of ev-ery best tra-di-tion

Leave the old gods": what ea-sy words to say!
from board-room power, or pop-u-lar ac-claim,
that noth-ing chan-ges, noth-ing can be done,
the Spir-it moves, and can-not be ig-nored.

How hard to move, with A-bra-ham's de-ci-sion,
and bear dis-com-fort, rid-i-cule, or mal-ice
we bear, like her, a prom-ise past con-ceiv-ing,
We feel the kick-ing of our in-ner vi-sion

break	free,	and	risk	a	new,	un -	cer -	tain	way.
with	earth's	di -	card - ed	peo -	ple,	in	God's		name!
of	jus -	tice,	joy,	sha -	lom,	and	king -	dom	come.
and	sing,	"My	soul	shall	mag -	ni -	fy	the	Lord!"

5 The voices from the past re-echo round us.
  Take courage from the faith of many friends.
  Go forth in faith, and look ahead to Jesus,
  on whom, from start to finish, faith depends.

6 With faith newborn, and passionate for justice,
  together now, we'll travel out from home,
  to sacrifice the peace of calm uprightness,
  and struggle for the city of Shalom.

Great Lover, Calling Us to Share

HAGEL
LM

1 Great Lov - er, call - ing us to share your joy in
2 Though sure of res - ur - rec - tion — grace, we ache for
3 Your quest - ing Spir - it longs to gain no sim - ple
4 As mid - wives who as - sist at birth, we give our
5 Self - giv - ing Lov - er, since you dare to join us

all cre - a - ted things, from a - tom — dance to
all earth's trou - bled lands and hold the plan - et
fish - ing ground for souls, but as life's sto - ry
ut - ter - most, yet grieve lest fol - ly, greed or
in our his - to - ry, em - brac - ing all our

ea - gles' wings, we come and go, to praise and care.
in our hands, a fra - gile, un - pro - tect - ed place.
on - ward rolls, a world more joy - ful and hu - mane.
hate should leave a spoiled, a - bort - ed, bar - ren earth.
des - ti - ny, we'll come and go with praise and care.

Text: Brian Wren, 1986. © 1989, Hope Publishing Co., Carol Stream, IL 60188. All rights reserved. Used by permission.
Music: William P. Rowan, 1988. © 1993, Selah Publishing Co., Inc. All rights reserved.

Here, Master, in this Quiet Place

QUIET PLACE
CM (86 86)

Unison

1 Here, Mas - ter, in this qui - et place, where an - y-one may kneel,
2 If pain of bod - y, stress of mind, de - stroys my in - ward peace,
3 If self up - on its sick - ness feeds and turns my life to gall,
4 You nev - er said "You ask too much" to an - y trou - bled soul.

I al - so come to ask for grace, be - liev - ing you can heal.
in prayer for oth - ers may I find the se - cret of re - lease.
let me not brood up - on my needs, but sim - ply tell you all.
I long to feel your heal - ing touch—will you not make me whole?

5 But if the thing I most desire
 is not your way for me,
 may faith, when tested in the fire,
 prove its integrity.

6 Of all my prayers, may this be chief:
 till faith is fully grown,
 Lord, disbelieve my unbelief,
 and claim me as your own.

Text: Fred Pratt Green, 1974. © 1974, Hope Publishing Co., Carol Stream, IL 60188. All rights reserved. Used by permission.
Music: William P. Rowan, 1983. © 1993, Selah Publishing Co., Inc. All rights reserved.

16

Hope Is a Star

SEYMOUR

Irregular with refrain

1 Hope is a star that shines in the night,
2 Peace is a rib - bon that cir - cles the earth,
3 Joy is a song that wel - comes the dawn,
4 Love is a flame that burns in our heart.
Refrain
lead - ing us on till the morn - ing is bright. When
giv - ing a prom - ise of safe - ty and worth.
tel - ling the world that the Sav - ior is born.
Je - sus has come and will nev - er de - part.
God is a child there's joy in our song. The last shall be first and the
weak shall be strong, and none shall be a - fraid.

Text: Brian Wren, 1987. © 1989, Hope Publishing Co, Carol Stream, IL 60188. All rights reserved. Used by permission.
Music: William P. Rowan, 1993. © 1993, Selah Publishing Co., Inc. All rights reserved.

How Blest Are They

SPLENDOR OF BELIEF

LM

1 How blest are they who trust in Christ when
2 In rip - ened age, their har - vest reaped, or
3 In Christ who tast - ed death for us, we

we and those we love must part; we yield them up, for
gone from us in youth or prime, in Christ they have e -
rise a - bove our na - tural grief, and wit - ness to a

go they must, but do not lose them from the heart.
ter - nal life, re - leased from all the bonds of time.
strick - en world the strength and splen - dor of be - lief.

How Shallow Former Shadows Seem

CARDINAL
CMD

1 How shal-low form-er shad-ows seem be - side this great re - verse, as
2 This is no mid-day fan - ta - sy, no flight of fe - vered brain. With
3 Yet deep with-in this dark-ness lives a Love so fierce and free that

Ped.

dark - ness swal - lows up the Light of all the u - ni - verse: cre -
ven - geance aw - ful, grim, and real, cha - os is come a - gain: the
arcs all voids and— risk su - preme!—em - brac - es ag - o - ny. Its

a - tion shiv - ers at the shock, the Tem - ple rends its veil, a
hands that formed us from the soil are nailed up - on the cross; the
per - fect tes - ta - ment is etched in i - ron, blood, and wood; with

pal - lid still - ness sti - fles time, and na - ture's mo - tions fail.
Word that gave us life and breath ex - pires in ut - ter loss.
awe we glimpse its true im - port and dare to call it

good.

I Come with Joy

TIMOTHY
86 86 6

1. I come with joy to meet my Lord, for-giv-en, loved, and free; in awe and won-der to re-call his life laid down for me, his life laid down for me.

2. I come with Chris-tians far and near to find, as all are fed, the new com-mu-ni-ty of love in Christ's com-mun-ion bread, in Christ's com-mun-ion bread.

3. As Christ breaks bread and bids us share, each proud di-vi-sion ends. The love that made us, makes us one, and stran-gers now are friends, and stran-gers now are friends.

4. And thus with joy we meet our Lord. His pres-ence, al-ways near, is in such friend-ship bet-ter known: we see and praise him here, we see and praise him here.

5. To-geth-er met, to-geth-er bound, we'll go our dif-ferent ways, and as his peo-ple in the world we'll live and speak his praise, we'll live and speak his praise.

If I Could Visit Bethlehem

SIMMONS
CM

1 If I could vis - it Beth - le - hem what pre - sents would I bring?
2 I would - n't take a mo - dern toy, but gold to pay for bread,
3 I'd learn some sim - ple words to speak in Ar - a - ma - ic tongue.
4 If Ma - ry asked me who I was and what her child would do,

If I could see what hap - pened then, what would I say or sing?
some wine to give his par - ents' joy and wool to warm his bed.
I'd cra - dle him, and kiss his cheek, and say, "I'm glad you've come."
I would - n't talk a - bout the cross, or tell her all I knew.

5 I'd say, "He'll never hurt or kill,
and joy will follow tears.
We'll know his name and love him still
in twenty hundred years."

6 I cannot visit Bethlehem,
But what I can, I'll do:
I'll love you, Jesus, as my friend,
and give my life to you.

Kneeling in the Garden Grass

Via Crucis

77 77 with refrain

Kneel - ing in the gar - den grass, Je - sus groans a -
I While the court and priests con - spire how to slant the
II When the mas - sive cross of wood bends and bruis - es
III Je - sus falls be - neath the weight of the cross he's

gainst his death, let this cup of sor - row pass, while he
ev - i - dence, Je - sus calm - ly bears their ire as his
Je - sus' frame, hear him seek e - ter - nal good as he
forced to bear, yet its load of sin and hate do not

prays in that same breath:
prayer grows more in - tense: not my will but yours be done.
prays in Yah - weh's name:
crush his hope and prayer:

Kneeling in the Garden Grass
(The Stations of the Cross)

I Jesus is condemned to death

While the court and priests conspire
how to slant the evidence,
Jesus calmly bears their ire
as his prayer grows more intense:
    not my will but yours be done.

II Jesus carries his Cross

When the massive cross of wood
bends and bruises Jesus' frame,
hear him seek eternal good
as he prays in Yahweh's name:
    not my will but yours be done.

III Jesus falls the first time

Jesus falls beneath the weight
of the cross he's forced to bear,
yet its load of sin and hate
do not crush his hope and prayer:
    not my will but yours be done.

IV Jesus meets his afflicted mother

Jesus reads in Mary's eyes
all the sorrow mothers bear,
and he prays his friend supplies
grace to strengthen her own prayer:
    not my will but yours be done.

**V Simon of Cyrene helps Jesus
to carry his Cross**

We with Simon of Cyrene
help the Savior bear the cross.
Step by step we slowly glean
what true faith and prayer will cost:
    not my will but yours be done.

VI Veronica wipes the face of Jesus

Seek the courage and the grace
that Veronica displays
when she wipes the bleeding face
of the one who bravely prays:
    not my will but yours be done.

VII Jesus falls the second time

Jesus trips and falls again
as he struggles through the street
where the mob's unceasing din
mocks the prayer his lips repeat:
    not my will but yours be done.

VIII Jesus meets the women of Jerusalem

Christ directs the women's tears
toward the coming judgment day
when God weighs our faithless years
with our willingness to pray:
    not my will but yours be done.

IX Jesus falls a third time .

Jesus stumbles one last time
nearly broken by the load
yet by prayer finds strength to climb
Calvary's final stretch of road:
    not my will but yours be done.

X Jesus is stripped of his clothes

Naked to the sun and clouds
and the jeers and gawking stare
of the soldiers and the crowds
Christ continues with his prayer:
    not my will but yours be done.

XI Jesus is nailed to the Cross

While the soldiers throw their dice
they ignore their victim's groans,
lost to them the sacrifice
and the prayer that Jesus moans:
    not my will but yours be done.

XII Jesus dies on the Cross

Jesus gives one loud last cry
at the moment of his death
while his prayer moves heaven's sky
with his final, parting breath:
    not my will but yours be done.

**XIII The body of Jesus is taken down
from the Cross**

As they take the body down
and they wrap it in a sheet
in their hearts they hear the sound
that his lips no more repeat:
    not my will but yours be done.

XIV Jesus is laid in the tomb

Quiet is the hollowed cave.
Peace and tears and grief descend.
Mourners offer at the grave
what they learned from Christ their friend:
    not my will but yours be done.

22

Long Ago, Prophets Knew

KOTAJÄRVI

666 66 with refrain

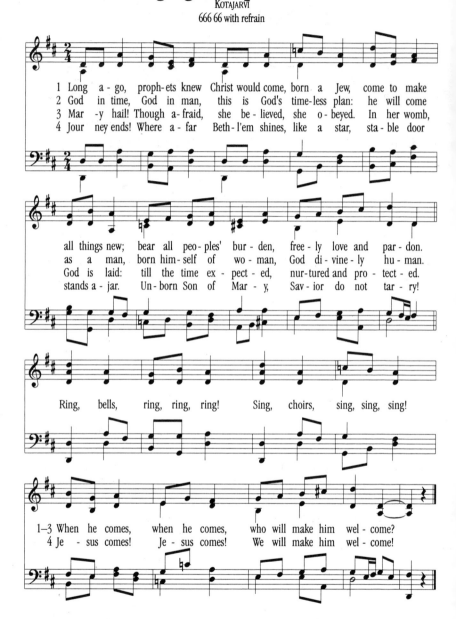

1 Long a - go, proph-ets knew Christ would come, born a Jew, come to make
2 God in time, God in man, this is God's time-less plan: he will come
3 Mar -y hail! Though a-fraid, she be - lieved, she o - beyed. In her womb,
4 Jour ney ends! Where a-far Beth-l'em shines, like a star, sta - ble door

all things new; bear all peo-ples' bur - den, free - ly love and par - don.
as a man, born him-self of wo - man, God di - vine - ly hu - man.
God is laid: till the time ex - pect - ed, nur-tured and pro - tect - ed.
stands a - jar. Un-born Son of Mar - y, Sav - ior do not tar - ry!

Ring, bells, ring, ring, ring! Sing, choirs, sing, sing, sing!

1–3 When he comes, when he comes, who will make him wel - come?
4 Je - sus comes! Je - sus comes! We will make him wel - come!

Text: Fred Pratt Green, 1971. © 1971, Hope Publishing Co., Carol Stream, IL 60188. All rights reserved. Used by permission.
Music: William P. Rowan, 1983. © 1993, Selah Publishing Co., Inc. All rights reserved.

Lord, Thank You for the Jews

STAR OF DAVID

Irregular

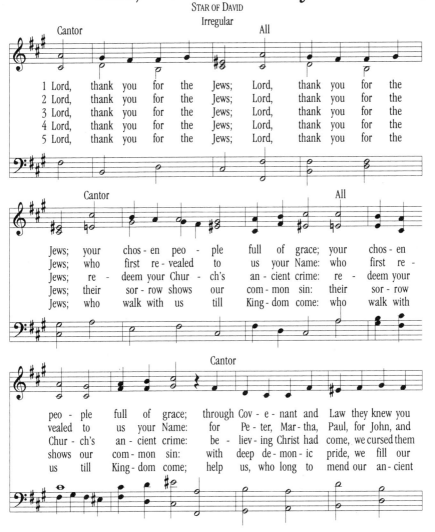

1 Lord, thank you for the Jews; Lord, thank you for the Jews; your chos - en peo - ple full of grace; your chos - en peo - ple full of grace; through Cov - e - nant and Law they knew you

2 Lord, thank you for the Jews; Lord, thank you for the Jews; who first re - vealed to us your Name: who first re - vealed to us your Name: for Pe - ter, Mar - tha, Paul, for John, and

3 Lord, thank you for the Jews; Lord, thank you for the Jews; re - deem your Chur - ch's an - cient crime: re - deem your Chur - ch's an - cient crime: be - liev - ing Christ had come, we cursed them

4 Lord, thank you for the Jews; Lord, thank you for the Jews; their sor - row shows our com - mon sin: their sor - row shows our com - mon sin: with deep de - mon - ic pride, we fill our

5 Lord, thank you for the Jews; Lord, thank you for the Jews; who walk with us till King - dom come: who walk with us till King - dom come; help us, who long to mend our an - cient

Text: Brian Wren, 1984.
Music: William P. Rowan, 1986.

first as ONE and LORD; in pro - phe - cy and praise they
Mar - y Mag - da - len, who prayed "Thy King - dom come" in
as for - ev - er wrong, through cen - tu - ries of hate that
world with sheep and goats and feed our self - es - teem by
part - ing of the ways, to re - cog - nize their faith, and

Cantor

wres - tled with your love through cen - tu - ries of test - ed faith, to
syn - a - gogue and home, and found you as they knew and loved a
paved the dev - il's way to Ausch - witz, and the Ho - lo - caust: how
do - ing oth - ers down, ap - plaud - ing "us" and curs - ing "them," like
ut - ter Je - sus' name, not in po - lem - ic, but in praise, till

All

be a light to all the world, to be a light to all the
Rab - bi out of Naz - a - reth, a Rab - bi out of Naz - a -
could your Chris - tians be so blind? how could your Chris - tians be so
crowds who mock the cru - ci - fied: like crowds who mock the cru - ci -
all our hopes are made com - plete, till all our hopes are made com -

1, 2 Cantor   All

1 world. Ho - san - na! Hal - le - lu - jah! Ho - san - na! Hal - le - lu - jah!
2 reth. Ho - san - na! Hal - le - lu - jah! Ho - san - na! Hal - le - lu - jah!

Lord of the Universe

STONEHENGE

10 10 10 10 10 with refrain

1 Lord of the u - ni - verse, hope of the world,
2 Lord of the u - ni - verse, hope of the world,
3 Lord of the u - ni - verse, hope of the world,
4 Lord of the u - ni - verse, hope of the world,

Lord of the lim - it - less reach - es of space,
Lord of the in - fi - nite e - ons of time,
send out your light to the ends of the earth.
how your cre - a - tion cries out for re - lease!

here on this plan - et you put on our flesh,
you came a - mong us, you lived our brief years,
May we who know you o - bey your com - mand,
looks for you, longs for you, watch - es and waits,

vast - ness con - fined in the womb of a maid;
tast - ed our griefs, our a - lone - ness, our fears,
go with the grace of your gos - pel to all,
prays for your king - dom of jus - tice and peace!

born in our like - ness you ran - somed our race:
con - quered our death, made e - ter - ni - ty ours:
bring - ing sal - va - tion and free - dom and joy:
Mak - er, Re - deem - er, tri - um - phant One, come!

Refrain

Sav - ior, we wor - ship you, praise and a - dore;

help us to hon - or you more and yet more,

help us to hon - or you more and yet more!

My Soul Proclaims with Wonder

HUNT

76 76 D with refrain

Refrain

My soul pro-claims with won-der the great-ness of the Lord;
re-joic-ing in God's good-ness my spir-it is re-stored.

1 To me has God shown fa-vor, to one the world thought frail,
2 God's mer-cy shields the faith-ful and saves them from de-feat
3 The migh-ty have been van-quished, the low-ly lift-ed up.
4 To Ab-ra-ham's de-scend-ants the Lord will stead-fast prove,

D.C.

and ev-ery age will e-cho the an-gel's first "All hail."
with strength that turns to scat-ter the proud in their con-ceit.
The hun-gry find a-bun-dance; the rich, an emp-ty cup.
for God has made with Is-rael a cov-en-ant of love.

Name of All Majesty

PATCHETT
66 64 D

1 Name of all maj - es - ty, fath - om - less mys - ter - y, King of the
2 Child of our des - ti - ny, God from e - ter - ni - ty, love of the
3 Sav - ior of Cal - va - ry, cost - li - est vic - to - ry, dark - ness de -
4 Source of all sov - 'reign - ty, light, im - mor - tal - i - ty, life ev - er -

a - ges by an - gels a - dored; power and au - thor - i - ty,
Fa - ther on sin - ners out - poured; see now what God has done
feat - ed and E - den re - stored; born as a man to die,
last - ing and heav - en as - sured; so with the ran - somed, we

splen - dor and dig - ni - ty, bow to his mas - ter - y—
send - ing his on - ly Son, Christ the be - lov - ed One—
nailed to a cross on high, cold in the grave to lie—
praise him e - ter - nal - ly, Christ in his maj - es - ty—

1-3   4

Je - sus is Lord!

No Iron Spike

LIVING CHRIST
LM

1 No ir - on spike, no gran - ite weight, no
2 Two nights he lay be - neath the earth, a
3 Be - fore dawn's mists could wreathe and coil and
4 Three wom - en came to hon - or Christ with

mob a - roused and crazed by hate could seal in stone to
hol - lowed rock his bor - rowed berth. Two nights it seemed death
lift the scent of clay and soil, God's fin - ger poked a -
pun - gent oils of herbs and spice. In - stead they found this

last - ing death the Christ who is our life and breath.
ruled the land; two nights and then death lost com - mand.
side the stone, and Christ a - rose to take his throne.
star - tling sight: a young man sit - ting robed in white.

*5 The words he spoke to Jesus' friends
are words of hope that God still sends
to those who grieve beside the grave
and ask if God can really save:

6 "The one you seek does not lie here.
Walk out in faith and not in fear,
and you will see beyond your loss
to Christ who lives despite the cross."

* stanza 5 is optional

O Christ, the Healer

HEALING CHRIST

LM

1 O Christ, the Heal - er, we have come to pray for health, to
2 From ev - ery ail - ment flesh en - dures our bod - ies clam - or
3 How strong, O Lord, are our de - sires, how weak our know - ledge
4 In con - flicts that de - stroy our health we rec - og - nize the
5 Grant that we all, made one in faith, in your com - mu - ni -

plead for friends. How can we fail to be re - stored, when
to be freed; yet in our hearts we would con - fess that
of our - selves! Re - lease in us those heal - ing truths un -
world's dis - ease; our com - mon life de - clares our ills. Is
ty may find the whole - ness that, en - rich - ing us, shall

1-4

reached by love that nev - er ends?
whole - ness is our deep - est need.
con - scious pride re - sists or shelves.
there no cure, O Christ, for these?

5

reach the whole of hu - man - kind.

O Joseph

CARPENTER

87 87

1 O Joseph, were you moved by her— moved by the maid - en Ma - ry? Yes, for com - pas - sion claimed your heart, al - though your mind was wa - ry!

2 O Joseph, did you hear of him— him of the Lord's be - get - ting? Yes, you o - beyed the an - gel's word, though dan - gers proved be - set - ting!

3 O Joseph, did you see him born— saw you the ho - ly birth - ing? Yes, and you took him as your son, though child of heav - en's earth - ing!

4 O Joseph, was the boy once left— left in the tem - ple quest - ing? Yes, and you found him find - ing God, with grace and growth a - test - ing!

5 O Joseph, sensed he then your love— love when he seemed a both - er. Yes, for he hon - ored love from you by call - ing God "our Fath - er!"

6 O Joseph, did you teach him wood—
taught you his first vocation?
Yes, and at length he took up wood
and crafted our salvation!

7 O Lord, could we be saints like him—
trusting, obedient, caring?
Yes, help our lives and lips proclaim
the tidings you came bearing!

Text: David A. Robb, 1985, ©.
Music: William P. Rowan, 1985. © 1993, Selah Publishing Co., Inc. All rights reserved.

Other Gospel There Is None

30

AGAPE
76 76

1 Oth - er gos - pel there is none than the one Christ gave us;
2 Love is ev - ery - where the same, sac - ri - fic - es, suf - fers;
3 Love is an - xious to a - tone, seeks for just de - ci - sions:
4 In God's King - dom all are one, when, in love, we share it:
5 In this spir - it we must strive for the world's sal - va - tion,

love it is, and love a - lone, has the power to save us.
love it is that bears our shame, love is what God of - fers.
love it is, and love a - lone, heals our deep di - vi - sions.
what ad - van - ces have been won through the Ho - ly Spir - it!
of - fering all we have to give with - out res - er - va - tion.

Text: Fred Pratt Green, 1980. © 1982, Hope Publishing Co, Carol Stream, IL 60188. All rights reserved. Used by permission.
Music: William P. Rowan, 1985. © 1993, Selah Publishing Co., Inc. All rights reserved.

Praise the God Who Changes Places

BOE

85 85 with refrain

1 Praise the God who chang - es plac - es, leaves the loft - y
2 Praise the Rab - bi, speak - ing, do - ing all that God in -
3 Praise the Breath of Love, whose free - dom spreads our wak - ing
4 Praise, un - til we join the sing - ing far be - yond our

seat, wel - comes us with warm em - brac - es, stoops to wash our
tends, dy - ing, ris - ing, faith re - new - ing, cal - ling us his
wings, lift - ing ev - ery blight and bur - den till the spir - it
sight, with the End - ing - and - Be - gin - ning, danc - ing in the

feet.
friends.   Stand   up,   friends!   Hold   your   heads
sings:
light.

high!   Free - dom is our song!   Al - le - lu - ia!

Text: Brian Wren, 1985.

Music: William P. Rowan, 1985.

Text and music © 1986, Hope Publishing Co., Carol Stream, IL 60188.

Praise the Living God Who Sings

SMITH
77 77 77 with alleluias

1 Praise the liv - ing God who sings, puls - ing through cre - a - ted things,
2 Christ was born and an - gels sang till the realms of hea - ven rang!
3 Rise to sing where there is wrong: "Truth and jus - tice have a song.
4 Cel - e - brate cre - a - tion's God! Mag - ni - fy re - demp - tion's Lord!

har - mon - iz - ing na - ture's arts, voic - ing hope in hu - man hearts!
Je - sus, God's own song on earth, sang of par - don, love, re - birth.
Let the bur - dened find re - lease; grant them free - dom, hope, and peace!"
Praise the Spir - it's power to bring un - der - stand - ing as we sing!

Al - le - lu - ia! Al - le - lu - ia! God's e - ter - nal an - them rings!
Al - le - lu - ia! Al - le - lu - ia! Christ who rose gives life new wings!
Al - le - lu - ia! Al - le - lu - ia! Seek the joy that jus - tice brings!
Al - le - lu - ia! Al - le - lu - ia! Wake the wood - winds, pipes, and strings!

Al - le - lu - ia! Al - le - lu - ia! Tell the na - tions God still sings!
Al - le - lu - ia! Al - le - lu - ia! Eas - ter peo - ple, God still sings!
Al - le - lu - ia! Al - le - lu - ia! Share the mes - sage God still sings!
Al - le - lu - ia! Al - le - lu - ia! Join the an - them God still sings!

Text: David A. Robb, 1985, ©.
Music: William P. Rowan, 1985. © 1993, Selah Publishing Co., Inc. All rights reserved.

Prophets Give Us Hope

PROPHETS
Peculiar

1 Proph - ets give us hope. They thirst for truth and right, and
2 Proph - ets give us truth. They come too close to home and
3 Proph - ets give us life. A - lone, yet not a - part, their

feel the pain of all dis - card - ed peo - ple, crushed, ig - nored, op -
show our word - y faith where love would take us if we dared to
quirks and fail - ings keep them ve - ry hu - man, sin - ners, yet for -

pressed. They give and get no rest, but stand a - gainst the powers - that - be as
go. We do not want to know, yet still they call us to de - cide: to
given. They are the Spir - it's leaven that makes our as - pir - a - tions rise, then

sign - posts of in - teg - ri - ty to point the way, and give us light.
ban - ish them, or take their side and set our sights on Christ a - lone.
gives, un - know - ing, as it dies, a taste of hope, a sing - ing heart.

Thank You, God, for Water, Soil, and Air

PENET
9 10 10 9

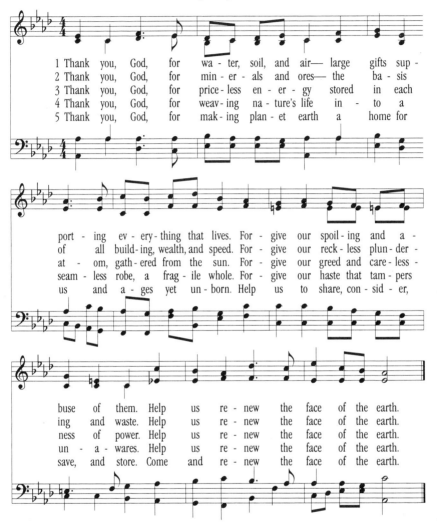

1 Thank you, God, for wa - ter, soil, and air— large gifts sup -
2 Thank you, God, for min - er - als and ores— the ba - sis
3 Thank you, God, for price - less en - er - gy stored in each
4 Thank you, God, for weav - ing na - ture's life in - to a
5 Thank you, God, for mak - ing plan - et earth a home for

port - ing ev - ery - thing that lives. For - give our spoil - ing and a -
of all build - ing, wealth, and speed. For - give our reck - less plun - der -
at - om, gath - ered from the sun. For - give our greed and care - less -
seam - less robe, a frag - ile whole. For - give our haste that tam - pers
us and a - ges yet un - born. Help us to share, con - sid - er,

buse of them. Help us re - new the face of the earth.
ing and waste. Help us re - new the face of the earth.
ness of power. Help us re - new the face of the earth.
un - a - wares. Help us re - new the face of the earth.
save, and store. Come and re - new the face of the earth.

35

The Horrors of Our Century

GOD IS THERE

86 86 86 86 86 86

1 The hor - rors of our cen - tu - ry have iced the wells of
2 By tor - ture, war and pov - er - ty, by flame and fir - ing
3 Yet if, made like some an - droid race, though warm with flesh and
4 And God is not an an - a - lyst, ob - serv - ing gain or
5 The fruits of know - ledge, plucked and prized, have scat - tered wide their

grief. We greet each new a - tro - ci - ty in
squad, for free - dom and de - moc - ra - cy, or
blood, our hap - py self, with smil - ing face, was
loss, but loves us to the ut - ter - most, and
seed: we are as gods, with o - pen eyes, for

Text: Brian Wren, 1982. © 1983, Hope Publishing Co., Carol Stream, IL 60188. All rights reserved. Used by permission.
Music: William P. Rowan, 1983, 1985. © 1993, Selah Publishing Co., Inc. All rights reserved.

froz - en dis - be - lief;   yet all the e - vil en - er - gies that
in the name of god,   God's im - age finds a thou-sand ways to
pro-grammed to be good,   and had no free - dom, see - ing wrong, to
suf - fers on a cross: for love comes not like Heads of State, in
shame or glo - ry freed,   and share, as mid- wives to our God, the

haunt the hu - man race   come not from a - lien gal - ax - ies, but
tor - ment or to kill,   and asks how love could jus - ti - fy its
choose it, or say no,   our praise would be a pup - pet song, and
power and glam - or known,   but as a los - er, des - o - late, in
pain of giv - ing birth   to faith's ful - fil - ment, mer - cy's child: new

from our in - ner space: and Ausch - witz and Hi -
ter - ri - ble free will: for Viet - nam and South
love an emp - ty show: Pol Pot and Sta - lin
an - guish, and a - lone: Gol - goth - a and the
heav - ens and new earth.   Come blow, you winds of

ro - shi - ma in - trude on ev - ery prayer with
Af - ri - ca will drive us back to prayer, as
are the cost of ev - ery will - ing prayer that
Emp - ty Tomb en - light - en ev - ery prayer when
Pen - te - cost! Let all the church - es dare to

shades that whis - per "Where is God? If on - ly God were there!"
vic - tims clam - or, "Where is God? If on - ly God were there!"
choos - es jus - tice, love and trust, and hopes that God is there.
faith dis - cov - ers: "There is God, and all of God is there!"
strug - gle, suf - fer, die with God, and show that God is there!

There's a Spirit in the Air

FREINER

77 77

1 There's a spir - it in the air, tell - ing Chris - tians
2 Lose your shy - ness, find your tongue, tell the world what
3 When be - liev - ers break the bread, when a hun - gry
4 Still the Spir - it gives us light, see - ing wrong and
5 When a stran - ger's not a - lone, where the home - less

ev - ery - where: "Praise the love that Christ re -
God has done: God in Christ has come to
child is fed, praise the love that Christ re -
set - ting right: God in Christ has come to
find a home, praise the love that Christ re -

vealed, liv - ing, work - ing in our world."
stay. Live to - mor - row's life to - day!
vealed, liv - ing, work - ing in our world.
stay. Live to - mor - row's life to - day!
vealed, liv - ing, work - ing in our world.

6 May the Spirit fill our praise,
guide our thoughts and change our ways.
God in Christ has come to stay.
Live tomorrow's life today!

7 There's a Spirit in the air
calling people everywhere;
praise the love that Christ revealed:
living, working in our world.

37 # These Things Did Thomas Count As Real

ECALEVOL

LM

1 These things did Thom - as count as real: the warmth of blood, the
2 The vi - sion of his skep - tic mind was keen e - nough to
3 His rea - soned cer - tain - ties de - nied that one could live when
4 May we, O God, by grace be - lieve and thus the ris - en

chill of steel, the grain of wood, the heft of stone, the
make him blind to an - y un - ex - pect - ed act too
one had died, un - til his fin - gers read like Braille the
Christ re - ceive, whose raw im - print - ed palms reached out and

last frail twitch of flesh and bone.
large for his small world of fact.
mark - ings of the spear and nail.
beck - oned Thom - as from his doubt.

The Word of God Was from the Start

VERBUM DEI

LM

1 The word of God was from the start. The word drove seas and land a - part. The word made rocks and liv - ing things. The word raised up and brought down kings.

2 The word be - came a child of earth. The word ar - rived through hu - man birth. The word like us was blood and bone. The word knew life as we have known.

3 The word of God was hu - man sized, the word by most un - rec - og - nized. The word by oth - ers was re - ceived. The word gave life when they be - lieved.

4 The word had first made flesh from sod, the word-made-flesh turned flesh toward God. The word is work - ing on flesh still. The word is spell - ing out God's will.

5 The word shall be our life and light. The word shall be our power and might. The word a - bove all wealth is priced. The word by name is Je - sus Christ.

This Is a Story Full of Love

TIMOTHY
86 86 6

6 Arising over earthly powers
our Savior has begun
to catch them in a web of love
and weave them into one,
and weave them into one.

7 Praise God, the Wisdom and the Word,
till all the world can see
that Jesus is the first and last,
the keystone and the key,
the keystone and the key.

Text: Brian Wren, 1985.
Music: William P. Rowan, 1985.

This Is the Threefold Truth

ST. CYRIL OF JERUSALEM
66 66 with refrain

1 This is the three-fold truth on which our faith de-pends;
2 Made sa-cred by long use, new-mint-ed for our time,
3 On this we fix our minds as, kneel-ing side by side,
4 By this we are up-held when doubt and grief as-sails
5 This is the three-fold truth which, if we hold it fast,

and with this joy-ful cry wor-ship be-gins and ends:
our lit-ur-gies sum up the hope we have in him:
we take the bread and wine from him, the Cru-ci-fied:
our Chris-tian for-ti-tude, and on-ly grace a-vails:
chang-es the world and us and brings us home at last.

Christ has died! Christ is
ris - en! Christ will come a - gain!

This We Can Do

DOBY
Peculiar

1 This we can do for jus - tice and for peace:
2 This we can do for jus - tice and for peace:
3 This we can do for jus - tice and for peace:
4 This we can do for jus - tice and for peace:
5 This we can do for jus - tice and for peace:

we can pray, and work to an - swer prayers that
we can give till ev - ery - one can take life
we can see and help our neigh - bors see— what
we can fight what - ev - er hurts and tram - ples
we can hope and ho - ping, stride a - long our

oth - er peo - ple say. This we can do in faith and
in their hands, and live. This we can do in love and
is, and what could be. This we can do with truth and
down, or hides the light. This we can do with strength and
way while oth - ers grope. This we can do till God makes

see   it through—for   Je - sus   is   a - live   to - day.
see   it through—for   Je - sus   is   a - live   to - day.
see   it through—for   Je - sus   is   a - live   to - day.
see   it through—for   Je - sus   is   a - live   to - day.
all   things new— for   Je - sus   is   a - live   to - day.

Through the Heart of Every City

42

TRUESDELL
87 87 D

1 Through the heart of ev - ery cit - y runs the flow of hu - man
2 Through the pass - ing gen - er - a - tions, in their spir - it, flesh, and
3 Through our wit - ness and our wor - ship, Je - sus, grant that we may

need. Mid this glass and steel are puls - ing smol - dering wick and dam - aged
bone, Je - sus Christ be - comes in - car - nate: ho - ly hearts are liv - ing
still hear the heart - beat of com - pas - sion call - ing us to do your

reed. Has our Church a word to of - fer, some hope shin - ing from our
stone, build-ing here a house of ref - uge as a tem - ple, as a
will. You, our vine, and we, your branch-es, dead - ened not by an - y

creed? Walk-ing through the con - crete fur - rows Je - sus sows the Word as seed.
home. So with-in the cit - y's shad - ow Je - sus' plant-ed Word has grown.
chill; work-ing for the fi - nal cit - y when the har - vest is ful - filled.

Text: Sylvia Dunstan, 1987. © 1990, G.I.A. Publications. Used by permission. All rights reserved.
Music: William P. Rowan, 1987. © 1993, Selah Publishing Co., Inc. All rights reserved.

To Mock Your Reign

SCHEUER
CMD

1 To mock your reign, O dear-est Lord, they made a crown of thorns; set
2 In mock ac-claim, O grac-ious Lord, they snatched a pur-ple cloak, your
3 A scep-tered reed, O pa-tient Lord, they thrust in-to your hand, and

you with taunts a-long the road, from which no one re-turns. They
pas-sion turned, for all they cared, in-to a sol-diers' joke. They
act-ed out their grim cha-rade to its ap-point-ed end. They

did not know, as we do now, how glo-rious is that crown; that
did not know, as we do now, that though we mer-it blame, you
did not know, as we do now, though em-pires rise and fall, your

thorns would flower up-on your brow, your sor-rows heal our own.
will your robe of mer-cy throw a-round our nak-ed shame.
king-dom shall not cease to grow till love em-brac-es all.

44 # View the Present through the Promise

RAICA

85 85 88 85

1 View the pres-ent through the prom-ise Christ will come a-gain.
2 Probe the pres-ent, with the prom-ise Christ will come a-gain.
3 Match the pres-ent with the prom-ise Christ will come a-gain.

Trust des-pite the deep'-ning dark-ness Christ will come a-gain.
Let your dai-ly ac-tions wit-ness Christ will come a-gain.
Make this hope your guid-ing prem-ise Christ will come a-gain.

Lift the world a-bove its griev-ing through your watch-ing and be-liev-ing
Let your lov-ing and your giv-ing and your jus-tice and for-giv-ing
Pat-tern all your cal-cu-la-ting and the world you are cre-a-ting

in the hope past hope's con-ceiv-ing: Christ will come a-gain.
be a sign to all the liv-ing: Christ will come a-gain.
to the ad-vent you are wait-ing: Christ will come a-gain.

When Christians Shared Agape Meals

TIMOTHY SQUARE

86 86 6

1 When Chris-tians shared a - ga - pe meals, O Lord, your Spir - it
2 We gath - er still for love e - vents, and cel - e - brate with
3 We clothe our faith and hope with love to meet our neigh-bors'
4 We al - so bring our bur - dens here and share them as we
5 Keep us in car - ing fel - low-ship, and help us to re -

came to bless and love the in - fant church which gath - ered
song the pil - grim-age our par - ents made to keep our
needs, and find that serv - ing you through them tran - scends our
feast; grant us, O Lord, the gifts and grace to be each
spond by liv - ing out the ban - quet feast u - nit - ed

in your name and set each heart a - flame!
peo - ple strong— and we would join the throng!
hu - man creeds, ful - fill - ing faith with deeds!
oth - er's priest through whom your love's re - leased!
by a bond in this world and be - yond!

Text: David A. Robb, 1985, ©.
Music: William P. Rowan, 1986. © 1993, Selah Publishing Co., Inc. All rights reserved.

When All Is Ended

YOGANANDA
10 10 10 with alleluias

1 When all is end - ed, time and trou - bles past,
2 As in the night, when light - ning flick - ers free,
3 A - gainst all hope, our wea - ry times have known
4 Then do not cheat the poor, who long for bread,

shall all be mend - ed, sin and death out - cast?
and gives a glimpse of dis - tant hill and tree,
wars end - ed, peace de - clared, com - pas - sion shown,
with dream-worlds in the sky or in the head,

In hope we sing, and hope to sing at
each flash of good dis - clos - es what will
great days of free - dom, ty - rants o - ver -
but sing of slaves set free, and chil - dren

last: Al - le - lu - ia, al - le - lu - ia!
be: Al - le - lu - ia, al - le - lu - ia!
thrown: Al - le - lu - ia, al - le - lu - ia!
fed: Al - le - lu - ia, al - le - lu - ia!

5 With earthy faith we sing a song of heaven:
all life fulfilled, all loved, all wrong forgiven.
Christ is our sign of hope, for Christ is risen:
Alleluia, alleluia!

6 With all creation, pain and anger past,
evil exhausted, love supreme at last,
alive in God, we'll sing an unsurpassed
Alleluia, alleluia!

When on Life a Darkness Falls

DROOPING SOULS
76 76 D

1 When on life a dark-ness falls, when the mist flows chill - ing,
2 When the dreams and vows of youth pain - ful - ly ac - cuse us,
3 Come and meet him, friend and Lord, through the gos - pel sto - ry:

paths and sign - posts lost in doubt, love - less, un - ful - fill - ing,
stab our con - science, steal our worth, Christ will not re - fuse us:
o - pen door to life and peace, win - dow in - to glo - ry.

reach us, Je - sus, from your cross, though we feel for - sak - en;
peace the world can - not pro - vide, dai - ly res - ur - rec - tion,
All who seek him, soon are found, made his close re - la - tion:

keep us through the ach - ing night till new dawns a - wak - en.
strong com - pan - ion at our side for each new di - rec - tion.
Christ our path - way, Christ our home, Christ our sure foun - da - tion!

"Whom Shall I Send?"

HEAR HIS VOICE

LM

1 "Whom shall I send?" our Mak - er cries; and man - y when they hear his voice are sure where their vo - ca - tion lies: but man - y shrink from such a choice.

2 For who can serve a God so pure, or claim to speak in such a Name, while doubt makes ev - ery step un - sure, and self con - fus - es ev - ery aim?

3 And yet, be - liev - ing he who calls knows what we are and still may be, our past de - feats, our fu - ture falls, we dare to an - swer: "Lord send me!"

4 Those whom he calls he pur - i - fies, and dai - ly gives us strength to bend our thoughts, our skills, our en - er - gies, and life it - self to this one end.

With Humble Justice Clad and Crowned

RUITER-FEENSTRA

LMD

1 With hum-ble jus-tice clad and crowned, the Christ of God will
2 The Word of truth will free th'op-pressed, and, just-ly judg-ing
3 As thun-der-clouds of love rain down life-giv-ing, u-ni-
4 Say not that jus-tice nev-er dawns, that peace on earth will

come a-gain and sing in ev-ery land on earth the
ev-ery need, will end the power of flaunt-ed wealth, and
ver-sal showers, the meek will rule, and thus re-deem earth's
nev-er come. The prom-ise shines from Beth-le-hem, for

song be-gun at Beth-le-hem, and jus-tice shall de-
cru-el, quiet, sys-tem-ic greed. The vi-o-lence of
high au-thor-i-ties and powers, as work-ers dance with
all, for-ev-er, like the sun. A-long the high-way

Text: Brian Wren, 1989. © 1993, Hope Publishing Co., Carol Stream, IL 60188. All rights reserved. Used by permission.
Music: William P. Rowan, 1990. © 1993, Selah Publishing Co., Inc. All rights reserved.

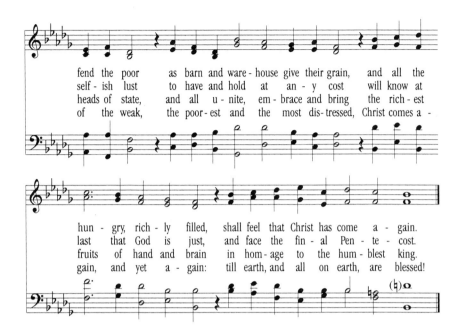

fend the poor as barn and ware - house give their grain, and all the
self - ish lust to have and hold at an - y cost will know at
heads of state, and all u - nite, em - brace and bring the rich - est
of the weak, the poor - est and the most dis- tressed, Christ comes a -

hun - gry, rich - ly filled, shall feel that Christ has come a - gain.
last that God is just, and face the fin - al Pen - te - cost.
fruits of hand and brain in hom- age to the hum - blest king.
gain, and yet a - gain: till earth, and all on earth, are blessed!

Woman in the Night

WICKLUND
55 55 with refrain

1 Wo - man in the night, spent from giv - ing birth,
2 Wo - man in the crowd, creep - ing up be - hind,
3 Wo - man at the well, ques - tion the Mes - siah;
4 Wo - man at the feast, let the righ - teous stare;

guard our pre - cious light: peace is on the earth!
touch - ing is al - lowed: seek and you will find!
find your friends and tell; drink your heart's de - sire!
come and go in peace; love him with your hair!

Refrain

Come and join the song, wo - men, chil - dren, men.

Je - sus makes us free to live a - gain!

5 Woman in the house,
  nurtured to be meek,
  leave your second place:
  listen, think, and speak!
Refrain

6 Women on the road,
  welcomed and restored,
  travel far and wide;
  witness to the Lord!
Refrain

7 Women on the hill,
  stand when men have fled!
  Christ needs loving still,
  though your hope is dead.
Refrain

8 Women in the dawn,
  care and spices bring;
  earliest to mourn;
  earliest to sing!
Refrain

Woman in the Night

WICKLUND
55 55 with refrain

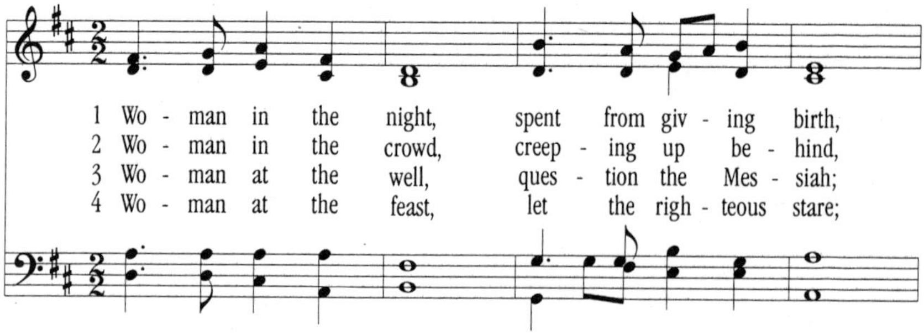

1 Wo - man in the night, spent from giv - ing birth,
2 Wo - man in the crowd, creep - ing up be - hind,
3 Wo - man at the well, ques - tion the Mes - siah;
4 Wo - man at the feast, let the righ - teous stare;

guard our pre - cious light: peace is on the earth!
touch - ing is al - lowed: seek and you will find!
find your friends and tell; drink your heart's de - sire!
come and go in peace; love him with your hair!

Refrain

Come and join the

Come and join the song,

Come and

Come and join the song, wo - men,

5 Woman in the house,
   nurtured to be meek,
   leave your second place:
   listen, think, and speak!
   Refrain

6 Women on the road,
   welcomed and restored,
   travel far and wide;
   witness to the Lord!
   Refrain

7 Womenn on the hill,
   stand when men have fled!
   Christ needs loving still,
   though your hope is dead.
   Refrain

8 Women in the dawn,
   care and spices bring;
   earliest to mourn;
   earliest to sing!!
   Refrain

You Made Your Human Family One

FAMILY
CMD

1 You made your hu-man fam-ily one, yet we are torn by strife,
2 Through-out this rich yet hun-gry world our plen-ty hides the poor,
3 Your sons and daugh-ters need your help where might and mon-ey reign,

as pow-er, pride, and pleas-ure join to mock the gift of life.
or we pass by in ap-a-thy and keep their needs ob-scure.
to shape a just and last-ing peace, with hu-man-kind hu-mane.

Let rea-soned pas-sion press for peace with faith that right will win,
Help us re-nounce the love of wealth and all self-cen-tered deeds;
To spare our frag-ile is-land home, we pray, "Thy will be done!"

as we wage love on war un-til your chil-dren live as kin.
help us ex-tend a wealth of love to meet our neigh-bors' needs.
Em-pow-er us to re-u-nite the fam-ily you made one!

Text: David A. Robb.
Music: William P. Rowan.

Topical index

Topical index

Scripture Reference

Exodus
4:13
God of many names

I Chronicles
16:42
When in our music, God is glorified

Psalm
72
With humble justice clad and crowned
102:1-7
O Christ, the Healer
150
When in our music, God is glorified

Proverbs
8:22-30
This is a story full of love

Isaiah
6:1-8
"Whom shall I send?"
11
Long ago, prophets knew
60:1-19
Arise, shine out, your light has come

Jeremiah
1:4-9
"Whom shall I send?"

Amos
6:1-7
O Christ, the Healer

Matthew
11:28-30
Come to me, O weary traveler
20:1-16
For the fruit of all creation
25:37-45
For the fruit of all creation

Mark
1:30-34
O Christ, the Healer
4:26-29
For the fruit of all creation
5:15
O Christ, the Healer
9:14-24
Here, Master, in this quiet place
14:26
When in our music, God is glorified

Luke
1-2
Long ago, prophets knew
8:43-48
Here, Master, in this quiet place

John
3:16
Other gospel there is none

Acts
1:9-11
Glorious the day

Romans
1:28-32
O Christ, the Healer
6:15-19
Glorious the day
8:31-39
How blest are they

Ephesians
1
Glorious the day
This is a story full of love
4
O Christ, the Healer
5:19-20
When in our music, God is glorified
6:9
For the fruit of all creation

Hebrews
1:1
Long ago, prophets knew

James
5:13-16
O Christ, the Healer

I Peter
1:6-7
Here, Master, in this quiet place

I John
4:-12
Other gospel there is none

Revelation
3:11
This is the threefold truth

Tune Names

Metrical Index—Tunes

CM (86 86)   QUIET PLACE

SIMMONS

CMD (86 86 D)   CARDINAL

FAMILY

SCHEUER

TRUESDELL

LM (88 88)   BATCHELOR

ECALEVOL

HAGEL

HEALING CHRIST

HEAR HIS VOICE

LIVING CHRIST

Metrical Index–Tunes

First Lines

Authors of Texts